The Young Riders
of Mongolia

Rob Waring, *Series Editor*

HEINLE
CENGAGE Learning™

Australia • Brazil • Japan • Korea • Mexico • Singapore • Spain • United Kingdom • United States

Words to Know

This story is set in Mongolia. It happens near Ulan Bator (ulan bɑtɔr), the capital city of Mongolia.

(A) **The Parts of a Horse.** Look at the picture. Write the letter of the correct word next to each definition.

1. the part of a horse's body that sticks out from the back: _____

2. the flat part of the face, above the eyes and below the hair: _____

3. the piece of hair that falls forward between a horse's ears: _____

4. the long body parts used for running and walking: _____

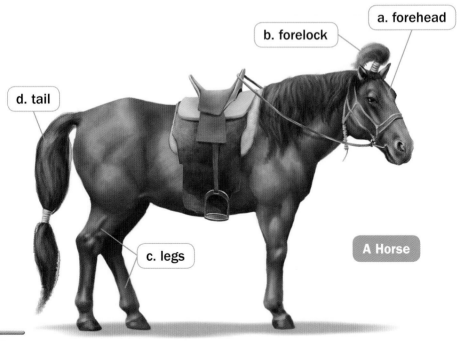

A Horse

B **An Old Tradition.** Read the paragraph. Then, complete the sentences.

This story is about an interesting horse race in Mongolia. In the race, the riders make their horses run very fast, or gallop. The fastest horse and rider wins the race. The race started in the 1200s, during the times of Genghis Khan. Genghis Khan was the emperor, or king, of a very big empire. Horses were very important in building his empire. He had a large cavalry with many excellent horsemen. Because of this, the sport of horseback riding continues to be very important to many Mongolians today.

1. People from Mongolia are called M_____ .

2. When horses run very fast they g_____ .

3. An event to see who is fastest is a r_____ .

4. An area ruled by one person is an e_____ .

5. The sport of riding horses is called h_____ r_____ .

6. The man who rules an empire is an e_____ .

7. A group of men who fight on horseback is a c_____ .

Genghis Khan
(c. 1162–1227)

A Horse and Rider

Mongolians are very good at horseback riding. People all over the world think that they're great horsemen. It's something that has always been a part of Mongolian culture, even in the 1200s. In the days of the emperor Genghis Khan, Mongolia had a very strong cavalry. This cavalry helped the emperor to create one of the largest empires ever known.

Since the days of Genghis Khan, life on the quiet **steppes**[1] of Mongolia has changed very little. Horses are still a very important part of the culture here. Many people often move from place to place. They need horses for their way of life, just as they did centuries ago.

---

[1]**steppe:** a large area of land with grass but no trees

 CD 2, Track 07

Long ago, Mongolia had a very strong cavalry.

In Mongolia, the people sometimes have events to show just how important horses are to them. Each year in July, thousands of people come from all over Mongolia to a place just outside the city of Ulan Bator. They come for the **festival**[2] of **Naadam**.[3] This festival has several important events in traditional Mongolian sports—including horseback riding. However, the Naadam race is a little unusual because the 'horsemen' at this event are just children. The riders must be less than 12 years old!

[2]**festival:** special day or time with special activities
[3]**Naadam:** [nɑdɑm]

What do you think?

1. Are there any festivals in your country?

2. What events do they have?

3. Are there any special activities especially
   for young people?

On the day of the race, careful and detailed preparations begin early in the morning. The horses have to look very special. The racers cover each horse's tail with **leather**.[4] They also cover the forelock on the horse's forehead. Then, people offer horse's milk to the spirits of nature. Horse's milk has an important meaning in Mongolian culture. After that, they use **incense**[5] to clean the area around the rider of bad spirits. Finally, they put a drop of this special milk near the legs to protect the rider and horse. At last the horses and riders are ready for the big race.

---

[4]**leather:** animal skin often used to make shoes
[5]**incense:** a substance that is burnt to produce a sweet smell

leather

Before the race, the parents of the young riders join them to walk around a special area. It's an important day and the mothers and fathers want to see the race. Every parent hopes that their child will be one of the winners.

It's a big event—about 500 riders will compete in the first race. It's a demanding event too; before the riders can even begin the race, they must walk the horses over **15 miles**[6] to the starting point.

---

[6]**15 miles:** 24.1 kilometers

Finally, the race begins. People wait at the finish line to watch the race. However, they can't see anything at first. The race is so long that it's actually happening miles away. The horses and riders are galloping towards the finish.

The viewers want to get near the winning horses. An old story says that the **dust**[7] that raises into the air when the horses run is special. People believe that it brings happiness and success to anybody it touches.

---

[7] **dust:** small, dry pieces of earth

After some time, the first horses and riders appear. It's been a very long race. These first riders have already been galloping for nearly 30 minutes!

The first five horses to finish the race will get a blue **sash**[8] for winning. The winners start to arrive, but the race won't finish for a long time. The other 500 or so horses and riders will keep coming in for another hour.

---

[8]**sash:** a long, thin piece of cloth

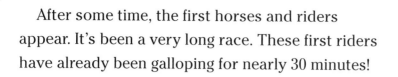

Identify the Main Ideas

Skim the story. Find three unusual things about the race at the Naadam Festival. Make a list.

The Naadam race finishes at the National Stadium, the country's main sports ground. There is a lovely party with a lot of music. A singer sings about the winning horses and how good they are. The winners walk around the sports ground. They're very pleased. They receive **medals**[9] and horse's milk.

---

[9]**medal:** a special circle of metal given to winners of a race

singer

It's the end of the Naadam race for another year. The race is very demanding for everyone involved. Indeed, these young riders are not just any children. They have shown their **skills**[10] in one of Mongolia's most important traditions. They've shown that they may just be the next great riders of Mongolia!

---

[10]**skill:** ability to do an activity or job well

After You Read

1. On page 4, 'they' in paragraph one refers to:
   A. people all over the world
   B. horsemen
   C. Mongolians
   D. horses

2. Today in Mongolia, _____ has changed since Genghis Khan.
   A. a lot
   B. little
   C. nothing
   D. everything

3. What is unusual about the riders in the festival of Naadam?
   A. They are good horsemen.
   B. They are Mongolians.
   C. They are women.
   D. They are children.

4. When is the festival of Naadam every year?
   A. January
   B. June
   C. July
   D. August

5. Which of the following is NOT part of preparing a horse for the festival?
   A. Incense cleans the area of bad spirits.
   B. The color of the tail is changed.
   C. The forelock is covered in leather.
   D. Horse's milk is offered to spirits.

6. On page 10, 'them' in paragraph one refers to:
   A. the riders
   B. the horses
   C. the parents
   D. the horses and riders

7. On page 13, the word 'begin' in paragraph one means:
   A. start
   B. do
   C. prepare
   D. join

8. People believe that the dust brings happiness to _____ it touches.
   A. nobody
   B. some people
   C. successful people
   D. anybody

9. What is a good heading for page 14?
   A. The First Riders Appear Quickly
   B. Riders Are Tired After the Horse Race
   C. A Very Long Race for the Young Riders
   D. Winners Come After One Hour

10. In the story, how do the young winners feel after the race?
    A. tired
    B. pleased
    C. young
    D. energetic

11. According to the story, what is one of Mongolia's most important traditions?
    A. creating empires
    B. drinking horse milk
    C. singing in the National Stadium
    D. horse racing

Genghis Khan

G enghis Khan was born in about 1165 in what is now called Mongolia. His life was not an easy one. His father was killed when Genghis was only nine years old. He then became responsible for his family. His mother taught him how to protect the family. This education was useful when he governed the empire that he created in later life. Genghis Khan was one of history's strongest leaders. He was responsible for bringing the Mongolian people together into a single nation. He achieved this by the time he was 30 years old.

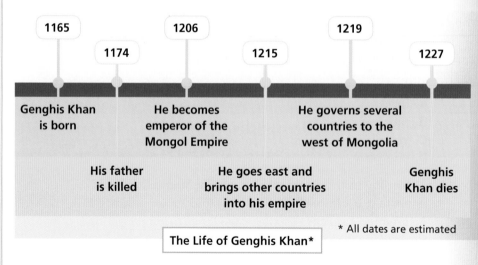

1165	1174	1206	1215	1219	1227
Genghis Khan is born	His father is killed	He becomes emperor of the Mongol Empire	He goes east and brings other countries into his empire	He governs several countries to the west of Mongolia	Genghis Khan dies

* All dates are estimated

The Life of Genghis Khan*

Genghis Khan learned to ride a horse at a very young age and he taught his men how to ride as well. Their horseback riding skills are well-known. His cavalry was one of the strongest and most fearless in the world. With the help of these men, this emperor changed Asia and the Middle East.

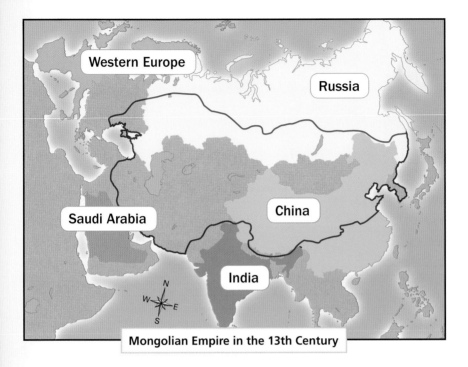

Mongolian Empire in the 13th Century

Genghis Khan created one of the largest empires in history. It started in Korea on the east and went all the way to Western Europe. During the Mongolian Wars, he and his calvalry moved across Asia and the Middle East. Khan then added each new country they entered to his empire. At one point, Khan's empire included parts of the countries we call China, Korea, Russia, and Mongolia.

Genghis Khan also achieved many other things. He set up the first trade agreements among the countries of Asia and the Middle East. He supported arts like painting. He even established a handwriting system for the Mongolian language. Over time, this led to increased trade and learning. To some people Genghis Khan was only a strong fighter, to others he was a lot more.

CD 2, Track 08

Word Count: 322
Time: _____

Vocabulary List

dust (13)
emperor (3, 4)
empire (3, 4)
festival (6, 15)
forehead (2, 9)
forelock (2, 9)
gallop (3, 14)
horseback riding (3, 4)
incense (9)
leather (9)
leg (2, 9)
medal (17)
Mongolian (3, 4, 6, 9)
race (3, 6, 9, 10, 13, 14, 17, 18)
sash (15)
skill (18)
steppe (4)
tail (2, 9)